Dear Wind, From Flower

K-poetry

SAEMMOON `1055`

Saemteo Lee Jeong-rok Poetry Collection

Red plum, you chatter among the snowflakes
with snow wind and snow flower

Your name is Red plum
You fill men's heart with excitement!

From ⟨Red Plum in the Snow⟩

The breath-taking heat
whether with eyes closed or open!
The rain that poured viciously
as if it's the end of the world
I guessed it would come slowly
But with the grumbling cry of cicadas
not knowing that the season has changed
Autumn has come with the desperate sound

From ⟨I Will Love in Autumn⟩

To the beings who are trembling in fear,
flap your wings like a swan
Pray like a saint
And dream like a fairy!

Drunk by her pheromone
Let's emit the superhuman hormone engraved in human genes
like a volcano
To defeat those evils

From ⟨Praying, White Magnolia⟩

Dear. _____

Date. _____

From. _____

Book publication `SAEMMOON`

Dear **Wind,**

From **Flower**

Best-seller Lady
-The lady came into my arms, making my heart tremble

The beauty and taste of poetry is quite bitter.
It went over the line of death.
It was free like a birdsong in a deserted forest.
It was lonely, but abundant.

The words that left me long ago,
the words that passed through so many things,
the words that have gone through years of dominant crossbreeding,
with swollen bellies, came into my arms and bore their babies.

Pain always comes before it is tamed.
Losing sorrow means losing love.
To confirm that I am alive
I will have to love all existences and suffer more.
A fearful, yet exciting best-seller!

It's only a beginning.
I would rather write a mind-touching poem than a well-written poem.
A poem that reflects the agonies of the era and nature,
a poem that contains the pain of the grass roots
a poem that possesses happiness inside.

Writer's Note

To present the heartbreaking lyrics to my readers
I will master my skills and proceed.
It's only when I jump over my standards and borders
will I see the new world of reasons.
I will always have the door open so poems can come to me.
It feels colder and sadder that we're losing the warmth among people than the cruel winter itself.
When everyone cowers, saying it's too tough a life,
from a distance, an apricot flower blooms its bud
and a fruit swells an inch more.

The swollen winds from the southern pacifics
have been visiting me lately to bear their children.
It's a tough time.
The pandemic still commands the world.
If such an insignificant, nano-meter wide creature is so strong,
then we, humans can command bigger things
like the heaven and earth, a greater universe.

We should cheer up.
Cheer up
and let go of your fear.
The strong wind blowing from the best-seller

will put this cruel disease to sleep.
The wind will extinguish it.
Let's cheer up!

To my loving family, friends, acquaintances,
and precious beings that I met on the path of literature,
those who support me with tears from a distance,
thank you all.
Thank you to my readers
who loved my humble works and gave me courage.
I will return it with good poetic works.

March 25, 2021
Saemteo Lee Jung-rok

SAEMMOON 1056

Dear Wind, From Flower
Lee Jung Rok - 10th Poetry Collection

Writer's Note : Best-seller Lady / 4

Part 1 Dear Wind, From Flower

/The Providence of Universe

Grab a drink with me / 14
Dream of the Blue / 15
Was it a Dream / 17
The Love of Stars / 19
The Theory of Revitalization / 21
The Theory of Health 101 / 23
A White Lie / 25
A Toast of Solitude / 26
Mother, Mother 3 / 27
The Clash of Ego / 31
Heaven and Hell / 32
The Law of Gravity / 34
Dear wind, From Flower / 36
Dream of a Creation / 38
Dream of Existences / 40

Part 2 The Love of Red Plum Blossoms

/The Mother Nature

Please Don't Forget / 44
A Lonely Autumn Night / 45
Dear Autumn Love / 46
Jewelweed / 47
I Will Love in Autumn / 48
Spring Cabbage Orgasm / 49
Spring Flower / 50
Magnificent View of Chuwolsan Mountain / 51
Love Song of the Dark Moon / 52
Breathtaking view of Damyang / 54
The Love of Red Plum Blossoms / 57
Praying, White Magnolia / 58
Red Plum in the Snow / 60
Life Dreams in Jungnangcheon / 62

Part 3   The Last Love that Remains on Land

/The History of Life

The News of Autumn / 64
Sweetbrier / 65
Summon the Lost World / 66
The Hub of Love / 68
Traumatic Life / 70
The Last Love that Remains on Land / 72
The Function of Alcohol and Love / 74
Let's Get Crazy / 76
Small But Definite Happiness / 80
Rice Water / 82
A Lunatic / 83
No Money, Long Life / 84
Putting Pieces Together / 86
Luck / 88
The Rule of the Sky / 89
Dear Trust / 90
The Husband I Promise To Be / 92

Part 4 My Love, Cry Baby

/Divine Love

The Husband I Promise To Be / 92
My Love, Cry Baby / 95
Paradise / 96
Divine Love / 98
She, the Angel of Our Star / 101
Strong Oath / 102
Our Love Story / 103
The Identity of a Gourd Flower 2 / 104
For the Glittering Love / 106
Mountain Peony / 107
Why Our Love Lasts a Thousand Years / 111
You Have Made It Well Until Now / 113
An Innocent Love Algebra / 115

Part 5 Severe Love

/Ego

Autumn Pain / 138
Cry, My Drink / 139
Market Day in Damyang / 141
Flowers That Did Not Bloom / 143
Flowers That Fell Before They Bloomed / 144
A Poet is a Martyr of Destroying Grammar / 145
Dear Heaven, Dear Heaven / 147
Full Moon on Chuseok / 149
Swan / 150
Moonlight Sonata / 151
Long Life Alone / 152
The Silver Grass Women / 155
Poem of a Smile / 157
Flapping the Skirt of the Robe / 159
Sinner / 161
The Lesson of Autumn / 163
The Landscape of Fairyland / 164

Part 6 Flapping the Skirt of the Robe

/Humor

Autumn Pain / 136
Cry, My Drink / 138
Market Day in Damyang / 140
Flowers That Did Not Bloom / 142
Flowers That Fell Before They Bloomed / 143
A Poet is a Martyr of Destroying Grammar / 144
Dear Heaven, Dear Heaven / 146
Full Moon on Chuseok / 148
Swan / 149
Moonlight Sonata / 150
Long Life Alone / 151
The Silver Grass Women / 154
Poem of a Smile / 156
Flapping the Skirt of the Robe / 158
Sinner / 160
The Lesson of Autumn / 162
The Landscape of Fairyland / 163

| The Providence of Universe |

Part 1.
Dear Wind, From Flower

Grab a drink with me

One glass for the snow
Another for the bitter life
For the love that melts my heart
And the cruel time
For the heartless friendship that leaves a sword scar

For this and that, let's grab a drink today
Today, we escape from the stiff heart
Our memories will blur and stop
We will be stuck in a groove
Today, I want to set back
the regret of the past with the fulfillment of present
Today, a chat with my friend becomes comfort
Today, I think of you with an empty heart

I've already had my drink
But I long for another
With excuses like this and that
Come and grab a drink with me

Dream of the Blue

Yang He Da Qu Jiu
is a prestigious liquor
produced in Yanghe, China, the heaven of drinks
by fermenting quality broomcorn, barley, wheat, and pea

Samteo, the poet,
could not make a living with his poems
So he owned a fashion business
in China for 20 years
In those days, he visited
the village of yunnan, a minority group
with Bang Seonghwa, the president of Chinese branch
In the summer afternoon, they shared lunch
when President Bang recommended
Haizhilan, a drink of 48 percent proof
The two finished the whole bottle of this hard liquor
Pulled off their clothes
And crossed the majestic Yangtze River

One day, President Bang
returned to his own country
to pay for the kindness of Samteo, the poet
for letting him run the Chinese business

He came to visit Samteo's living room
with another bottle of Haizhilan
And this time, along with a bottle of
'Tenzhilan,' more valuable than the former

The two met at a sashimi place that evening
With a plate of flatheat mullet, they finished both bottles
As dinner approached its end,
President Bang, as if planning to kill the poet,
brought up another bottle of liquor

Out of his suitcase
the label says, 'Meng Zhi lan(Dream of the Blue)'
This one is twice more expensive
than the Tenzhilan
And is 60 percent proof

That day, the two men finished
all three prestigious liquors
Flew up to Namsan Tower, Lotte Tower
And headed to Han River
Pulled off their clothes again
And swam all night long

  * Samteo: Poet Lee Jung-Rok's pen name

Was it a Dream
— A spell that expels the youth

Why is it
that we fear our mistakes of yesterday and today
Look at the beautiful fields and mountains, rivers and oceans,
and the time and space decorated with lights
Say farewell to the world with a glass of drink
and reflect on our dream of success and great work

The places where our eyes and footsteps stop at
All are our successful works
Why is it that we dwell on the victory or defeat
and the judgments of our future generations?
The horse with paper, pen, and ink in its mouth
and a sword and armor on its body
Its appearance was beautiful
but its glory was only an instant
No one would remember

It's already travelled a thousand miles
You cannot reflect your past, even on a bronze mirror
In the riverside, where apricot flowers used to bloom
and larks used to sing the songs of love,

only the waning moon hangs plaintively
Where has the silvery waxing moon gone?
Only the giant snakes jump up in shock

The historical sky
cannot stop the wind on a rainy night
Time cannot abandon the old stormy dream,
and is still keeping it in its heart

The days when I rarely got drunk
I looked down on the world with pride
But in a twinkle of an eye, everything became gray ash
And it faded away
The appearance of a hero, in my prime days
I have abandoned it all
Now I'm flowing with dust, gotten wet by snowflakes

The Love of Stars
– The Triangle of nidana, nostalgia, and connection

Countless stars are born in this Universe
They fuse, expand, and are separated by death
The harmony between the generation and extinction of
the Universe
What existence manages it all?
Are there omnipotent gods?
Does the humanity's law of connection
exist in or apply to those stars?
This is an eternal topic and question for the humanity

On the Earth
countless combinations of elements appear
They exist and fade away

The precious connection of a seed
requires the process of
soil, water, and sunlight gathering and shooting out a bud

The invaluable connection of a fish
is that it can only exist
with water, oxygen, and a large school of plankton

The nidana of humanity
is the essence of a bright, clear, and fragrant life
a faithful personality towards individuals
expressing love for each other
through an honest, cheerful, and thick story

The definition of an ideal nidana
is to empty one's heart first
Abandon the nature of pursuing greed
And starting from an artruistic heart
With a sense of sympathy
And the virtue of tolerance and consideration
Don't you think the nidana is maintained
through the value of this universal reasoning?

Human beings are a small universe
Each individual is an assembly of elements
In other words, everyone who passes by
is a star, comet, and planet
Our birth, encounter, fusion and expansion
separation by death,
love,
and the quarrel between a couple
These are the war of stars
The love of stars
And the fixed nidana that we cannot undo

The Theory of Revitalization

How to live long
is the humanity's forever question and longing
If we get a supernatural power
It can't be better

To do this, we bring back the story
The Theory of Revitalization
Revitalization is
taking care of your life
Raising, improving, reinforcing, and finding the way of life, and caring for hygiene

It's not confined to the masters of nirvana
who pursue eternal life
or supernatural powers
That is a misconception
If you care for revitalization at your youth
You rarely get sick, and you have a healthy body, heart, and image

The way to raise a healthy life
is not so difficult

Along with cultivating your character and image,
it's conforming with the law of nature

A person's figure depends on it
Life handles it and relies on it
Strive to revitalize your force, spirit, and body
These things lack, and you will get sick
If you lose them, you will get weak
If you run out of them, your life will end

Force is the basis of your body
Spirit controls your body
Figure is the house where your body lives

If you overly use your body, you will lack
If you exhaust your force, you will be dried up
If you exhaust your spirit, your life will be severed

And so, humans
Let's revitalize our force, spirit, and body
Preserve our character and life
And live out our span of life

The Theory of Health 101

Exercise is an important part of your life
Let's spare time for it
Or else, illnesses will take your time
Let's allow our body to the time
Exercise makes your day short
But makes your life long

A plate tilted
cannot store water at a heavy rain
But a plate left upright
gets full at a light rain
A well-built body will store time
and be filled with long life

Leave your ears open
So you can hear beautiful songs
Do not store all that you hear
Filter it out
So you can keep healthy emotions

Open your eyes
So you can see the beautiful scenes

Don't try to stuff everything you see
Filter it out
So you can keep the clean image

Autumn ripes
And our longing deepens
We long for a desperate love
Healthy love that travels a thousand miles
Live forever long!

A White Lie

It's not a red lie
You look like an angel with a beautiful figure
You're beautiful

I mean it
You're a kind-hearted angel
You're so beautiful

You're the best in the world
This sentence
I want to keep in my mouth

[Quotations by Samteo]

Great is a mother's nature
She's like an absolute being
Pulling and embracing like a black hall in the universe

When the heaven and earth are created
Even with the strong wind sweeping the universe
A mother is an absolute protector
keeping her nest and children

A Toast of Solitude

Pressing my voice distorted with despair
My cries toward the world
Kneel, step aside, and struggle

What in the high place
presses my voice with its weight?
The sound that twists and weighs down my body and heart
Is it the weight of my lost love?
Is it the limit of reality?
What is it?
How heavy it is!

My swollen heart can't handle it all
It cries out inside the tired glass
A solitude crying without a sound

To wake up hope from the long long darkness
I've fixed a glass of bomb cocktail for myself
I shake it to create a waterspout
Propose a silent toast, preparing for a new journey
I drink up the surging glass

Mother, Mother 3

⟨1⟩
The legend of inheritance
- Mother, you're beautiful by your name

The scent of golden field blowing in the autumn
is the scent of my mother's sweat
Her rough hands are her love
fixing food for us eight children
Her bent back
is the weight condensed with her sorrowful life

The paddy field of an autumn evening
Rice drooping, making crisp sounds
Sounds like my mother's autumn harvest
It makes my heart burn

The period of Japanese colonization
Independence
Memory of the Korean War
During that turbulent time
Under the slogan 'Let's live well'
She buckled up her belt
Bore, raised, fed, and taught eight children
And for fourteen years

she nursed our grandmother
Touched the hearts of many people
And was rewarded as 'a devoted daughter-in-law'
by the governor of her province

Farming the paddy fields
Chopping firewood
Crafting hairbrushes out of oak
Making bamboo baskets
Making hand fans
Calculating
Taking part in the new-village movement
Exchanging labors for family events
As the eldest daughter-in-law
She took care of 15 ancestral rites a year
As a homemaker, she cooked and washed the clothes
Managed all the housework
And helped my father's work

She bore, raised, and taught
She kept the side of her children
She watched them get married
Our mother
Now our mother became a legend
Mother, mother
Are legends only born from sorrow and hard work?
Like mother, like son
Now I'm writing one, too
Is this a sort of inheritance?

⟨2⟩
Hands of an angel

I miss the hands of the angel more and more
It's a hectic life
As it gets more tiring and exhausting
I'm more desperate to be in the arms of the angel

Before she became an angel
The year when she became 91
With a faint memory
Skipping letters
The angel called out the names
of her children, daughters and sons in law, and grandchildren

That year, on Chuseok
She could not recognize her own children
She would ask "Who are you?"
The angel suffered from the symptoms of dementia
She would lie on her side
call out "Lord, lord"
and "Mother, mother"

Her muscles and bones weakened
Even at her children's slight touch
She would cry "Ouch, ouch"
Pouring out burning pain
She could not sit, walk, or crawl
An angel wearing a diaper

This foolish son
After the angel left for the starland
Still ache in his hands, feet, and heart
And my pain reaches the sky

⟨3⟩
The land of angels

My mother, who raised her kids
like a flower in the field of the world, and a bright light
You are greater
than any existence in the universe
The greatest one, my mother
You exist and breathe forever
Mother, you are beautiful by your name

I'm always embarrassed before you
I will not speak of my being unfilial
Mother, mother
I ask for your forgiveness

Let me pay my debt
in my afterlife
Mother, mother
Please be happy in the land of angels

The Clash of Ego

That man has two universes
in one soul

In one universe
Countless star flowers bloom
In the other universe
Cruel solitude lies

Countless star flowers bloom and fade
Countless laughters become cries
Countless sorrows become joys

What is glorious in your universe
is disgrace in mine
So stop insulting the shared image
The two men quarrel

Dear god who reigns over the two universes
Please cure them
The two souls who clash over everything
Let them embrace each other and cry together

Heaven and Hell

Some people say
Heaven and Hell
are only a sheet of paper apart
We haven't been to any of them
We don't know yet

A virgin says
She went to Hong Kong 3 months ago
When he should have indulged on the delicacies of Hong Kong
He scattered seeds on the field, for no use

The single man says
He fought in a holy war 2 months and a few days ago
He traveled from Heaven and Hell
Worshipping his love
In return, he manured her field

The god says
Stay in dignity and self-content
And your world will be Heaven
Trapped in greed, stubbornness, and prejudice

Your life will be forever Hell
Pupil, do you understand?

The pupil of the god answers
"Master, I can't hold this question anymore
Whose seed is the virgin bearing?
Is it the single man's seed?
I do not have a clue"

"Pupil, when humans
come and go from Heaven to Hell
This man and that man
peek at this woman and that woman
It gets confusing
Okay?"

The Law of Gravity

I said no
Geumsook from next door, a year older than me
She likes me so much
Called me out to Gilgon's bamboo field on Chuseok
Holding my hands, she said

"When we become 20
You'll be a father, and I'll be a mother
So even if that fox living across the town
wags her tail at you
do not be tempted
Don't lose your mind, cause if you do
It will be life or death for you"

So I said, I can't
without Geumsook's permission
I said no and I refused
I shouldn't have carried the hairbrush for my father's errand

The girl said she'd moved from the sea
Like a sweetbrier, she was smaller than a milk vetch

She was as thin as a grass flower
She spoke quietly like a lark
That small girl
Pulled me towards her with arms stronger than the moon

Her temptation was so powerful
My heart, hard as a stone,
accelerated to worship her
from Heaven to Hell, Hell to Heaven
And a world was created in her temple

Dear wind, From Flower

The reason I love the wind
is because it shakes my heart

The reason the wind loves me
is because my figure shakes

The reason I'm weak at the wind's temptation
is because it takes away my heart

The reason the wind is weak at my temptation
is because my flowers are radiant

If I fall, I will be sad
So wind, please pass by me

When the rain beats me, it's so cold and sad
If you beat me, I will be left in pain and sorrow
Please just pass by me

When you roll a scroll of clouds
I send a ray of bright moonlight to you

My shaking heart
trying to love the starlight smiling with its eyes
Wind, come back and shake me

Under the dazzling sunlight
In your arms
Let me breathe

Before the sun sets
Before my petals fade

Love me
Love me
Wind, love me

Dream of a Creation

Looking at the golden morning sunlight
I had a random thought

The god went to conquer the Sun on a spaceship
but he melted like wax
Sucked up into a black hall, and was extinguished
Not only the god died
but all his legends broke down
It's a bitter story

In the generation of Science
the legends of gods have faded away
Have our dreams become happier?

Will those dreams surpass the phenomenal world?
Will they open the door of perception?
Will they enter the absolute world, the domain of gods?

A god, too, gets greedy and makes mistakes
Is this greed or challenge?
Should we, creations of the god, mimic his doing?

The Sun of yesterday and the Sun of this morning
are not much different
But the world has changed so much

With random thoughts passing this morning, I smile
Outside the window is sunny and bright
It's sprinkling the legends gathered from the gods
As if telling us to dream of symbiosis

Dream of Existences

A land unconquered
even by powerful nations or imperialists
No one can claim its territory

Its origin traces back to humanitarianism
With the identity of good will, the people restore their nature
And live the life of ego

They comply with the law of nature
And all objects, animals, and creations
live a life of symbiosis

Overcoming the source of humanity's pain and misfortune
Overcoming the weakness and ignorance of oneself
Conquering the limitations and incompetences
We live peacefully and harmoniously on this land

On this land
We do not live to pass an exam
or become a judge, prosecutor,
or a doctor, high-ranking officials

We live to express our talents
Develop, polish, and create
our specialized, deepened abilities
Filled with educational methods and practices
focused on self-development

On this land
We will not prioritize
our titles or ranks
We will strive for efficiency
of achieving unity through serving each other

On this land
Beauties like
art, humanities,
music, fine art, and literature
will not be chosen by the status or money
They will be enjoyed upon free will
and given opportunities
according to each person's capabilities

On this land
Labor will not be about making life
It will be the ground of opportunities
where we master and express ourselves
to create skills and develop our potentials

Labor will contribute by supplying physical energy
required for an individual and family's life
and the talents needed at work

On this land
The ideologies and binary thinking
tangled with competition, fight, politics, and wars
Black and white or camps will disappear or be purified
All relationships will cooperate to bring progress
Win-win through coexistence
They will be transcended
to the relationship of brothers and companions
Relationship of good will

| The Mother Nature |

Part 2
The Love of Red Plum Blossoms

Please Don't Forget
- A Thousand Years of Love

The crimson sunset bears a ripple
The river harvests time
The weedy swamp
is the green hope of a leaf attempting to fly
banished by deep envy

A forget-me-not bloomed
with purple intimacy along the waves
Desperate hope curdled
praying to sway and love forever

The glow of the setting sun
has fiercely eaten up the time
Blooming purple star flowers to live a sorrowful life

The porcupine island
lights up the flower lantern, opening the sky of a forget-me-not
Winding up a purple [1]binyeo around the falling moonlight
As the cluster of stars fade and dew flowers bloom

---

1) Binyeo: Korean traditional hair pin

A Lonely Autumn Night

What's the point of talking of the past?
Crossing the forest where a scops owl hoots
Moonlight flows through the sparse holes along the stone wall
Fables hanging on the trees

Cold breeze blowing for many days
Today, gray and wet fog sways
Spraying rain
The autumn raindrops draw my heart
because of the lonely longing

Starlight pours and rain drops tremble
Your moon is fading
Stormy wind shakes the forest
And the moonlight trembles like love in the past
What an autumn night

Dear Autumn Love

The tiny wild flowers presenting faint excitement
Toddling baby maple leaves lightly tinted
The shyness of a pomegranate
greeting with babies in her wide breast
The secret love of reeds
growing thick along the flower river
The innocent love of silver grass fluttering in the field

Under the autumn sunset
We all become lovers
It's a sorrowful autumn
A tough journey of pandemic and economy
Still, let's live through it
say the autumn lives colored in brown red
celebrating the season

My dears, today again
let's not bring shame to the heartaching newborns
Let's stand honorably
Protecting, consoling each other
so we can bloom laughters with joy and health

Jewelweed

Her angel wings are widely open
Pink pistil burning autumn light
Mountains and fields burning red
Cherry salmon tracing up the current
I'm drunk with the smile of the Aria

Autumn stories filling up her heart
On the nails of the leaves and toenails of the trees
On the water scales of the river
Autumn tints its color

Drawing a red spot on the white cloud
Drawing a pink line and coloring it
For the desperate lover
She writes a splendid poem

I Will Love in Autumn

Over the grass leaves lying on the ground
In the arms of the wet dawn dew
Autumn has come

The hysteria of the tropical night
Barely sleeping with the air conditioner on
We still have stories left from that short summer night
But in the arms of the cool breeze in morning and night
Autumn has come

The breath-taking heat
whether with eyes closed or open!
The rain that poured viciously
as if it's the end of the world
I guessed it would come slowly
But with the grumbling cry of cicadas
not knowing that the season has changed
Autumn has come with the desperate sound

You and I will sit in a cafe
enjoying the scent of tea and view
Talking of love for each other
Autumn has finally come

Spring Cabbage Orgasm

The naughty snow cover
releases the lust that existed
within the ego of a clear, white snow flower
caressing the blue skin

Around noon on a Lunar New Year's Day
To sneak at the affair
that determines their unfortunate fate
I jump over the bank of the vegetable garden

Orgasm welling up
The snow cover vomits all that is left of his lust
Exhausted without a remain
And returns to the hexagon snow country

A warm breeze of passion blows
The young lady who suffered a morning sickness
blooms a snow flower
in her deep womb

The weak, green leaf
slowly stretches its arms
and adjusts the spring sunlight

Spring Flower

I found a spring flower
But all it shows is a ripple on the river

I ask the lark, and it says
She woke up the spring sun who had fallen into a nap
Hopped on the aquamarine Gan-a-dang river
To see the red plum blossoms lighting a spring fire
Blowing the reed flute, tootle-too!

I asked the cuckoo, and it says
She grabbed the waist of the spring breeze, screaming with laughter
Hopped on the bamboo raft
To see the red jindallae lighting a spring fire
Blowing the wheat flute, tootle-too!

* Ripple : The glittering of moonlight and sunlight on water
* Jindallae : Azalea
* Gan-a-dang : A deep river in between Hoguk Temple and Bamboo craft shop located in the upstream of Youngsan River, Damyang, Korea

⟨It's a magnificent view of a temple, gazebo, cliff, bamboo field, bamboo craft shop, tamarisk, hundred-year-old trees, and 500-year-old Japanese hackberry creating a harmony⟩

Magnificent View of Chuwolsan Mountain

The bird calls filling up Chuwolsan Mountain
In Lake Damyang at the start of Youngsan River
The light of the mountain reflected on the crimson water
A [2)]jjokbae walks in flower shoes

Along the lengthening furrow of late spring
The [3)]Arirang melody stretches with sorrow
The [4)]si-gim-sae melody falls over the lake
Chuwolsan mountain, shining the light of sunset, peach flowers ripen red

When dusk falls
Moonlight more tender than the skin of a mountain girl
Plays tag with the starlight along the rapids of Youngsan River
A scops owl cries with sorrow
for the long path before the traveler

---

2) Small traditional boat of Korea
3) Korean traditional song
4) A specific note made in a Korean traditional song

Love Song of the Dark Moon

The night, when fallen leaves get moist by the dew
You walk past the Gan-a-dang of Wandong valley
Holding hands and chattering across the bamboo road
And sitting on the wall of the thatched cottage

As you open the field gate, the star light follows
And sits on the bamboo bench
But you only give a peek
And coldly walk away

In the early evening, You light up Youngsan River under the Yanggak Mountain
circling the pagoda of Hoguk temple
The temple bell cries at your sorrowful story

Strong wind sweeps the guardian tree of Wandong valley
Your appearance from behind looks bright and lonely
as you walk across the cloud bridge with a pack on your back

You pour moonwater on the thirsty rain-fed field of our village president

And at dawn, I cannot find you
as you drink bamboo wine and chat
with Queen Phallus Luteus at the village foreman's bamboo patch

The scholar of Wandong valley becomes the main persona of a sad love story
Staying up through this lonely, heart-breaking night
Missing his lover with an aching heart
Waiting for you to come

Breathtaking view of Damyang

The scent of a thousand-year-old pine flower at Sigyeongjeong
Gathering its hands while burning an incense
The poet at Songgangjeong blooms as a black apricot flower
Welcoming bees and butterflies

Chuwolsan, the origin of Youngsan River
Where the heavenly flowers bloom
Kkachibong Peak, where the magpies lay their eggs
Jangwonbong Peak, full of integrity, setting up a folding screen
The clear but simple cottage of Yangsanbo and gazebo in Sosaewon
Resemble the phoenix sitting over a Firmiana simplex

The remains of wind and frost flow along the stream
Dust falls down with the time
Moonlight comes into the Jewoldang house
And into the breast of winter jasmine
Into the skirt of water lillies
And hangs over the purple eyelash of Byeogodong

Sipping tea with Maehyang
And falls asleep

Moonlight shining brightly along the dreams
Past Chuseong village and the beautiful mountains
Covering the universe
Returns before Maehyang wakes up
And falls asleep in the dew of bamboo leaves
It's a dew that embraces the universe
The poet names it bamboo tea
And pours it into a bottle

Thoughts covered with moss
I should wash it in the river colored by beautiful ixeris!
Or wash it in the scent of bamboo blowing from the forest!
In between the looks of the dew water
I hear the voice of Yangsanbo
I will quietly approach the skirt of hibiscus
blooming in the pond
Fishing love
And fishing time

* Sosaewon: Korea's first garden in Damyang, South Jeolla province

* Jewoldang: A gazebo in Sosaewon where guests chat and read books - The name means 'welcoming moonlight'

* Yangsanbo(1503-1557): A scholar that lived in Joseon Dynasty who once passed the state examination, but gave up the honor and lived in solitude after Purge of 1519

The Love of Red Plum Blossoms

Along the current of Youngsan River
Along the melody of Gan-a-dang waterlight
The sound of opening
the fragrant crimson breast

Under the moist sunlight of her first period
Her nipple flowers, like my shy sister
The wind in heat tries to pull off her clothes
The curious scent
The lady of lust

When the snow field felt a grief
And the sediments of rapids melted down
The snow flower became a legend

On the sunny hill where larks lay their babies
The scent of a shepherd's purse passes my nose
The day when haze flatters
The passionate red love is beautiful

Flapping the red skirt
The lady walking in flower shoes
The new wife, red plum blossom

Praying, White Magnolia

The warm spring light tickles me
When I stand in front of her white smile
My mind becomes clear

Under the golden sunlight
When she flaps her wings
She becomes a heavenly swan

Under the silvery moonlight
When she prays
She becomes a saint in a temple

Under the starlight of a blue house
When she dreams
She becomes a fairy

Curious of what is
inside her white skirt
When I approached her
I fainted away

If I presented an armful of

her innocent smell to the world
Would the cruel, filthy virus
be cleared away?
In the flowery road
We should all hold our hands and walk together
The world is ours
But what are we afraid of?

With her pure smile
We should clear human beings' hearts
And purify the nature
But why is it so hard?

To the beings who are trembling in fear,
flap your wings like a swan
Pray like a saint
And dream like a fairy!

Drunk by her pheromone
Let's emit the superhuman hormone engraved in human genes
like a volcano
To defeat those evils

Red Plum in the Snow

[1]
The lady misses the snow flower embracing her like a man
Her moist inner skin is fragrant
And her red lips are sensuous

The man caresses her
From joint to joint of her naked body
And in between the fetters
The lady chatters all night long

Lady of lust
Pops her scarlet lips and tints
the snow flower that looks into her eyes bloody red

The man cannot sleep
And the green posts dream on this winter night
Drunk by her scent
And by her red lips

[2]
The flower bud rises from the snowflakes
Blooming nervously

Red plum, you chatter among the snowflakes
with snow wind and snow flower

Your name is Red plum
You fill men's heart with excitement!

Life Dreams in Jungnangcheon

The rose forest where fancy display stands lie
Their red, pink, and yellow tentacles
tempt the men passing by
It's a covenant ceremony of blood

On a lonesome rock
A family of mallards taking a walk and relaxing
Teaching their kids to dive for natural food
Along the thin, long trail
The spring sunlight walks in meditation

When May, the queen of seasons
harvest the day and rolls it up
to load on a carrier

'Stealing the spotlight!'

A family of hairy crab out for a picnic
On the mat
Raises their robotic arms
Threatening the queen to unroll the mat
So they can dry their bodies

They make the queen speechless
After being so late

|The History of Life|

Part 3

The Last Love that Remains on Land

The News of Autumn

I heard that you got drunk
Gone on a bender
I heard that the drink made you cry
You sobbed your heart out

I heard that you became ripe
Ripe with sweet scent
I heard that the sweetness made you cry
You cried out loudly

I heard you were overjoyed with the change of color
You were sad with the change of color
It's autumn
Saying hello to you

Sweetbrier

I tear up with the longing for you
You're a thousand miles away
About to return to me
Rain cloud with its swollen belly
About to give birth
The gourd-flower lady on the roof
About to build the moon

The Gwangalli beach after a thousand miles of walk
On the sandy beach
You become red
And I become an entomophilous flower
Pollinating passionately

All over your branches
Newborns have come into bearing

Summon the Lost World

The cord of remains flutters in the snow wind
The white string dances
On the land where white anonymous flowers pile up
I paint sunlight over sunlight
filled up with snowflakes
The frost of snow flower calls back the memories
And enters them on a fine nano-chip flower bud

I download
The face that I once deleted
The name that once left me
The pain that froze up
The longing covered with moonlight and starlight

In the snowy forest
I have a time of my own
when I can face myself
And meet another part of myself
And call a person that I long to meet

The night when silvery moonlight pours down
Let's write down the serenade of moonlight blue

that flower buds dance to and the wind sings of
Let's recite and save it

On the moon flower grown by the forest fairy
On the star flower grown by the legend of the wilderness
On the platform of your heart
that is nitrated, where I can access with warmth
Let's input the white world
so we can summon it anytime

The Hub of Love

Seed-line, vertical-line, and life-line sway
A leash, school-tie, regionalism, marriage, and love come untied
White string is about to go to the underworld along the snow wind

Mountain field where anonymous flowers pile up white
Let's format everything clean
By blowing ten thousand strings of sunlight
to the frozen heart of the land

While snow frost forms up
Let's summon the memories through the reflecting light
And insert them into the flower bud nano-chip

Let's download
The sorrowful story
The frozen pain
And the pity laid over a moon flower

Within the time when I face myself in the white forest
Into the arms of peace and silence

Let's invite the ones we long to meet

With the seranade just for you
conducted by the forest scent and sung by the birds
Let's invite the love string

In your heart where we can access
Like a warm, new floor
Let's build a hub

Traumatic Life

As we live our lives
Three things can never return
Time, word, and chance

There are three things you must keep
Hope, gratitude, and honesty

The three most precious things are
Love, friend, and confidence

The three keys to success are
Diligence, effort, and passion

The three things that destroy a person are
Pride, greed, and anger

As we live our lives,
luxuries are valuable yet needless
But a mop
is necessary for everyone

There are three types of people

Foolish, dull,
and wise

The foolish do not recognize a relationship
The dull cannot keep a relationship
The wise makes a relationship even at a slight chance

Where does the difference come from?
In his life,
a person is affected by
who he meets,
what book he reads,
which mentor he meets,
and what kind of love he receives

As someone says,
It's better late than never
As I decide to renewal my life
I blush up, as if innovation starts from my face
And my heart beats up fast
It's the beginning of a remodeling
It's a trauma

The Last Love that Remains on Land

The seed sprinkled aloof
Blooms wide as a flower
The sweet scent should wake up the world
But look at the sunlight
The gray grimace
Refusing the bloom its bud

The tree rooted down with all its might
It must be green and fresh
But look at the forest
It's like a traveler with brown rags on
Groaning

The energy of the nature
Must heal the tired hearts
But look at the sky
With the absence of moon and stars
The village has disappeared

The forest where time has stopped
Anxiety fills the air

Listen to the weeping of plants and trees
Spirits suffering from the diseases
The tinkling of wind-bells and the bier
Emptying the birds' nests

Humans are toxic
They exhaust the energy
They are a goner who have abandoned their nature
A paradox that has lost ration and compliance

What should we do
to circulate the time that once stopped?
To summon the objects that are absent
and revive the dying lives?
Don't we need the water of life?

Humans, be concious
Let's go back to our nature
The warm tears
shed by realizing our nature
will become the water of life
that wets the nature's thirsty throat

The Function of Alcohol and Love

On a depressing day
It makes me feel better
But sometimes, it makes me feel sad
That's when I want it more

Yes,
Love is the same

When my head aches
A lonesome drink makes me more lonely
When I remove the foam
It shows its real face
Then, I want to take it back

Yes,
Love is the same

It makes me confident
and say the truth
It's even happier when it comes back
How sad it is
when I only give, but don't receive

After I enjoy it, it's the end and meaningless

Yes,
Love is the same

It's a cat-and-mouse game
I find it on a tiring, sad day
But it makes life harder as I rely on it more
It helps me forget things
But at times, it's only a pretend

Yes, yes
Love is the same
That love was the same

It's toxic at first
The later you learn it, the better
Obsession will only make you sick

Hahaha
Funny how
It resembles my old love

Let's Get Crazy

Let's get crazy for just one year
Just one year is enough
Carpe Diem,
Getting crazy means
You try your best in one thing
with a dream, passion, and love

Get crazy for just one year
And your life can change
Set a goal, and get crazy
You'll see yourself different

Make thorough plans
And in your heart
Have trust and confidence in yourself
If you don't act fiercely
You won't gain anything
Success is given to those who take a challenge

Take a challenge
With trust in yourself
Success is not about luck

You discover
the way to success
because you got crazy with a goal, trust, and passion

To make success
You need to reflect on yourself
Know what you want
And set your goal in line with it
If you choose what you really want
It increases the possibility for you to succeed
and live a happier life

The thing that determines
whether you succeed or not
is how much hope you have
And how fierce your passion is
Prepare what you need in advance
Clarify your goals
And have trust and confidence
It will give you a legend of success

You need positive energy
Depending on your thoughts and emotions
You will have different energy
Collect more success assets of your own
The success asset will help you break through

All circumstances with wisdom

Make your plans thorough
Set goals that you will pursue for one year
And get crazy with that work
It all depends on you
Depending on how determined you are
It can make nothing or everything
Practice makes another practice
You should put it to a start
Seize an opportunity when it comes to you
And put it into practice

These are how you put it into practice
Be diligent
Do it with all your might
Don't be afraid of failures
Have strong belief in yourself
Don't jump into conclusions

You only know whether it's success of failure
after you try it
You also gain chance from a failure

Cherish people around you
Have a sense of challenge

Set long-term goals

Small practice changes your habits
New habits change your fate
If you want to taste the sweet fruit of success
One year, get crazy for just one year
Your friends will call you 'a retard' many times
But that's what makes you foolishly happy
Let's get crazy together!

Small But Definite Happiness

In our lives
small objects and events
bring us comfort
Happiness earned from tiny things,
sewing clothes
digging up herbs
cooking dishes
picking gray hair on your husband's head
massaging your wife's exhausted legs
throwing a coin to a beggar
making kimchi
for an old lady next door who lives alone
drawing a caricature for your loved ones
blushing at an erotic drama
shedding tear at the scene of breaking up
getting touched by small heroic actions

From these simple things
we gain peace and happiness
Living a simple life means
moving from your head to heart

Live from your heart
Think less
Be less sensitive
And be less logical

When you live from your heart
You will feel more of small happiness
Your life itself will become a joy
At last, you will achieve your life

Rice Water

Simmering gently, what a beauty
It looks good when it overflows

Thanks to your overflowing consideration
Your overflowing generosity
Your overflowing love
It's time to fill up our stomachs

It's the gift from God
The water of life, flame, and grains
simmer inside you
My heart is filled with happiness

A Lunatic

An algorithm of innovation

Everything in life has its own way
To bear good fruits
Fruits of high completeness
We must commit our passion
With speed and acuracy

But the foolish beings
Repeat the same thing every day
And wait for a different result
Wait for a good result

If you want a different result
If you want to harvest quality fruits
You must change your way of doing it
You must innovate it

No Money, Long Life

Whether you want to keep what you have
Or dream of earning a fortune at once
Your clothes, food, and house are the 3 elements of life
All three, you cannot have without money
Money is essential to live a happy life
But don't be servile in front of money
Don't be proud
Money is not a pushover which you can look down on

Some people gain money one day
And keep it for the rest of their lives
Others, in just one day,
lose what they have accumulated for all their lives
Money has bright eyes, and is cold and stern
It's beyond our imaginations

When you have nine, you want to make it ten
That is human lust
If you can't control your lust
When you catch a get-rich-quick fever
You only get empty-handed regrets and tears

Those who dreamed of getting rich at once
End up empty-handed in their final years
That's the common law of economic justice
So lock up your lust
Open your heart with compassion for others when you have the honor
Don't go too far

Putting Pieces Together

The sorrowful bridge that we cross in our lives, without a speech
The images that have broken and shattered apart
With an empty heart, I draw it in my mind to put them together
Drawing, erasing, putting them together, and undoing it
The small island that you left with me
I sweep it and let it root down in the sky
Blooming its flower

The porcupine island, embracing the scar, dreams a dream
The humpback whale
summons the mermaid to a silver wave
The devil ray
pulls up the longing that has been thrown in the sea
searching for the source of the deep sea

The love I did not reach in life
In case I get bruises in my heart
The lonely sea draws it in solitude, holding fear
Loneliness swallows the island

Life is yet to judge
You have to live it till the end
to learn that your will can't make it all
The porcupine searching for food
The story of whales and shrimps tingling with one another
and the desperate love of a mermaid

Let's hold onto the seed-line fixed into our hearts
And put the pieces together like Arachne
The colorful pieces

Luck

Preparation is the seed and foundation stone of hope
waiting for happiness to come
If the fairy of luck cannot find the stepping stones
She will change the direction
And go somewhere else

The luck that comes to you
is not at all, a coincidence
Interestingly, it's the best present
that inevitably comes to those who are prepared

Don't get obsessed with how you look
Rather, refine your beautiful spirit and pure heart
When you meet a dharma friend and give it a touch,
It will bloom as a shiny flower

The Rule of the Sky

Watched the same phenomenon
from the same spot
But the feelings and emotions
vary by person

We all have our bias
Like bionovular twins
who live in the mother's womb for months
but cannot come to the world at once

The cycle of seasons
starts from one point
and returns to the same point
But there is no such thing as
the same spring, summer, autumn, and winter
It's mysterious love
And compliance to the rule of the sky

Dear Trust

Dear Trust
Committing yourself to others
means to comfort the incomplete being
and love the way it is

Dear Trust
When you wet things with truthful tears
and melt them with your smile
The spirit of commitment bears power of change
and creats a magical relationship

That is
your great love

| Divine Love |

Part 4
My Love, Cry Baby

The Husband I Promise To Be

On a day of large snowflakes
For you, who comes home late after work
I'll prepare a warm bag of sweet potatoes
and a red umbrella
I'll wait for you in front of the tree house door

You can come into the tree house
And rest your body and mind
I'll prepare a living room
full of phytoncide smell

Sometimes, I'll be a husband
who prepares a meal of savory dwenjang soup
with bamboo shoot and bean sprouts
and white steamed rice made of lotus pip and yam seeds

When you stay up late in the study room
composing a desperate love poem
I'll fix herb tea
with my love added inside

I'll be your closest friend

Quietly standing next to you
I'll be a husband
whom you can share your poetic stories with
I'll be your lover
who loves you till death
I'll be a husband
like clean air
that makes you breathe

I want to live like this
And if, in this tough world
I get to leave you alone
and set off on a far journey to star land
I'll still be a husband
who always carries you in the heart
comforting you and loving you

If you and I meet again in next life
Love again till death
And fade away as a star flower of star land
Holding hands, closing our eyes

"I was happy to meet you and love you
in my former life and current life
When I arrive at another star land
I'll build a tree house for you again"

I will be a husband
who can promise to you
and give you the last kiss

My Love, Cry Baby

When things pass by, let them pass
When things come, let them come
Leave your heart open

If it's false, say it is false
If it's true, say it is true
If you like it, say you like it
If it's love, love till death
But if you are still lonely and desperate
Have some silent moment
And give a smile of tears

Life is, life is
Meant to be like that
It's meant to be like a cry baby's heart

Paradise

⟨1⟩
I will sing my love for you

You are my soul
My heaven
Within you, I abide

Oh~ you are my universe
My star land
Within you, I fly

Oh~ you are the break of my soul
The peace of my heart
You are my mission to live

I'm a shepherd planting star in the star field
You are the shiny star flower

With your eyes
Shine me brightly

Song, oh shepherd's song

Song of the star flower

⟨2⟩
I will sing for your soul

You are my pain
My joy
Within you, I abide

Oh~ you are my prison
My maze
Within you, I live eternally

Oh~ you are the comfort of my soul
The healing of my heart
You are my desperate fate

I'm a shepherd leading the moon in night sky
You are the smiling moon flower

With your love
Shine me brightly

Oh song, a shepherd's song
Song of the moon flower

Divine Love

The lights that I collected in my heart
Sunlight, starlight, and moonlight
Have bloomed as beautiful flowers
I scan the scenery with the eyes of my heart
And send it to you

The longing that I grew with care
The obedience of pure love
I will tune it with the frequency of your soul
And send it to you

These are ornaments
or fancy accessories
that can bless your Christmas
with beauty and warmth
Next to you who will drink a toast
I will stand with a candle
and pray

Among these objets made for our happiness
If you need anything more
I'll be happy to give what I have left

I hope you can use all I have
Within the divine light and silvery wave of the hymns
lighting the church decorated with love
When the jingle bell rings
I will see you with warm tears

My only wish is, after the divine festival
If you could sense
my desperate longing
It's from my long long wait
So please let it touch your heart and give you joy

This Christmas is filled with cruel wind
blowing from the pandemic
If we can defeat it with our abundant love
I will become a candle melting hot
And by your window
I will stand all night long

Like this, you are alive in my heart
You are the reason I live
I thank God for sending you to me
And I worship Him

For our dream, passion, and love
Let's drink a toast of wine more beautiful than blood
Let it be a toast of blessing
Just for you

She, the Angel of Our Star

There's something about Gwangalli
A thousand miles feel so close
Her smile is the magic of shortening distance

There's something about Songdo
Countless time feels so short
Her wink is a time machine

There's something about Haeundae
Long night doesn't feel so lonely
Her arms are the heaven flowing with honey

When I talk to her, I hear her laughter
Rather than an answer, her wide smile
Hugs me wide

Did the angels return to star land?
Or did they retire?
She became the angel of our star

Strong Oath

The road in the sky isn't a single path
Sometimes, the cloud sets it apart
Other times, the lightning and storm divides it

The road which you and I take together
Same rule applies
Sometimes, there is another path for detour
My love, take the other path

When human beings think of one path
They can create ten other paths
After they pick the stars, they want to plant them
And bloom more star flowers

Is it our greed?
It's a talent granted by God!
Until death seperates us
I want to be lost in your maze
LIke our strong oath

Our Love Story

The light coming from the floating moon
Is brighter than ever
There is a star flower that blooms vividly
only in complete darkness

We, lovers, are standing in the night sky
We whisper to each other, wetting the moonlight
Moonlight is so short
Star flowers fold their tassels
It's red dawn

The morning sea curls
The midwife wakes up the newborn sun
slapping its bottom
The world wakes up
And our love has woken up

Praying for each other's peace
We read the letter of our hearts
The lighthouse leads our way
It protects our love

The Identity of a Gourd Flower 2

⟨1⟩
A vine spread out from the heart patch of our nation
It bloomed in the early autumn field
Its sad smile holding the white sorrowful beauty
Keeps the emotion of white nation
The longing from deep inside ripens
And bears a white fruit round as breasts

The woman's heart growing along the fence of the mountain field
Blooms abundant emotions
Mountain ridge goes along with the curve
A white candle plump like a moon jar sits on the roof
Red chili lying on the table
tints the clear sky
And the woman's heart flies up to the divine sky

⟨2⟩
The woman's heart empties her womb and becomes a bowl
It's a thousand-year-old tool used by our nation
It is plain, simple, but somewhat pretty
It makes my heart swell up

Water fills up to its brim
Grains swarm inside
Poverty scratches it hard
Turning it into a gourd mask
Used to drive out evil spirits
or bring out joy and humor

Or else
It fills various lives in its empty womb
Repeating pregnancy and birth
Keeping things alive, healing, and reproducing

With the form of pur love and obedience
With the emotion of closeness and abundance
Making itself a divine symbol of life
I want to meet the woman's heart

For the Glittering Love

Let's not think about the one who left
Let's love the one who came

In this glittering flower garden
let's welcome the wind, sunlight, and dew

Let's forget the regret and scratches
Let's squeeze the pimples out

New wind and sunlight have come
Let's embrace the new visitors
It's a joy of picking stars every day

Mountain Peony

[1]
One night, I had a dream
With a desperate move
Holding the shoulders of a shabby man
A woman, smiling wide

With a quiet, excited smile
Full of the autumn's light
On the night of cold heart
The woman came into my arms with passion

Trying to hug me with weak tentacles
With her bitter scent
The lovely woman
welcomed me with her wide smile

[2]
Another night, I had a dream again
In the Church where we pray with hands clasped
Just breathing and relaxing with her
was ardent happiness

You, whom I enjoy and adore with abundant love
When one of your stars and one of my stars
paint the night blue with glittering eyes
You're a saint with a lamp on your heart and hands
put together
You make a divine move
and a plaintive smile
You pray with tears in your eyes
and dream of the light of silent night sea
You, my love

[3]
On a past night, I had a dream again
On days I suffered from wounds of the past
Sadness I shed in my eyes
You ceased it with your white smile

I long to see you, though I am looking at you
I want to see you again
You make my heart tremble with love
I long to see you
You make me stay up late with longing

I plant you in my yard
And manure you with my innocence
You bloom your white flower
My love, you

[4]
Last night, I had a dream again
A dawn embracing sunlight
The fresh and clear scent
You make me start my day

We talk about stories of life
Cry and laugh together
consoling each other
You and I are partners of life
walking the path of mission

You are my only flower
You always bloom beautiful flowers like a dream
And look at me with a white smile
My love, you

[5]
Tonight, I will dream again
I will give you my life
so you can bloom the one flower
in your deep heart and spirit
I will pray for you

And if,
we become apart in this life

I still loved you till the end of this world
With a sorrowful smile
And tearful eyes
My heart will ache with longing for you

You are in front of me, but I long for you
I am looking at you, but I long for you more
You are the one true love of my world
And I want to give you happiness for sure
So, you are a forever flower
My love, you

Why Our Love Lasts a Thousand Years

Dear my love
From the grave that wandered as a light in the water
You survived as a brilliant soul
And returned as my precious one

Dear my love
You wandered in the river of death to search for longing
And found a stone built with the spirit of former life
And returned with sorrow

Dear my love
You lived well
And thanks for coming to me
I waited a thousand years for you to come

Did you know that?
Our love lives and longs for a thousand years
Our love dies and longs for a thousand years
That is how deep our love is
Our love is so strong
that it touches our spirit

[Quotations by Samteo]

A flower is...

The flower of love is infinite
It travels from life to death
Sublimates into a piece of light
And pierces the heart of its lover
It blooms from the aching heart

You Have Made It Well Until Now

You are so weak
But you crossed the bloody river of countless hardships
You have chewed on your bitter courage
And with much effort
You have made it well until now

I, who have been here sorrowfully alone
can't thank you more
My life has been hard, fearful, and risky
No one would listen to our words
Stories that could not be solved
But those moments, painful like hell
Are passing by

You and I
Though our hearts are torn and aching
That must not be it!
Let's get rid of the solitude and fierce loneliness
And with an open heart like the sky
With embracing movements like the wind
The longing, love, and happiness that touch our skin

Let's grab them tight
Alright, you?

You and I
Our wandering was tough and desperate
The road of hardship was so painful
But it wasn't a wrong path
Do you agree?

You have made it well until now
It's the blessing from God
Well done
Thank you
I give you comfort and praise
You have made it well
I feel thanks to you
I love you until death
I love you

An Innocent Love Algebra

All people
dream of a special love
We dream that an angel-like lover
would come, riding a cloud

But love only occurs
when innocent beings
open their hearts to each other
And the moment of loving, and being loved
is when we are truly alive and breathing

Being loved
is an incident of burning a fire
But loving someone
is becoming a legend
that lights up with oil that would not dry up

A being who only cares to be loved
is a candlelight fading out
A being who cares to love others
is an ever-burning light of legend

[Quotations by Samteo]

Humans dream of love
since the beginning of their lives

A dream of being loved
lasts shortly like a candle

A dream of giving love to others
is an infinite light
that holds the spirit of the world's beginning

| Ego |

Part 5
Severe Love

Frost Flower
— A sorrowful love

On the cozy cabin
Which the summit of Halla Mountain embraces
The sky pours blessings

The white snow that Baengnokdam holds
Empties the world clean
like the pure heart of an innocent girl

On a peaceful night like this
I want to drink a thick cup of coffee
Pour milk into hot espresso
And draw a heart shape

The deep coffee scent
Tickles the snowflakes
And my thick longing for you sits on the windowsill
Embroidering white star flowers

Do you hear that?
The frost lower
crying with longing for you

Bamboo Drink, the Scent of a Hermit

Green energy covering up
the bamboo forest, where the souls of scholars remain
Tears of integrity dangling on the leaves
The cry of a cuckoo is sorrowful
The moon, hanging on the bamboo branch
Flows and sinks into clear dew

A dogmatic ritual that has been awaited for a hundred years
Spirits of the bamboo forest bloom the bamboo flowers
Drawing up dew from bamboo roots that held legends
The ripening sound of the yeast in bamboo drink
that heals an exhausted body and soul

On a night that has swallowed the solitude
Remains of the past days
when it moisted thirsty souls
Revealing their wounds
And touching their souls with the bamboo scent
The bamboo drink consoles and heals the souls

An Inn in Juknokwon

Where old maids of Wandong valley tie up ribbons with a fine-comb
Where scholars of Hyangyo Cave draw the Four Gracious Plants on a bamboo branch
I want to be there in Juknokwon

Where bluebirds and the scent of bamboo dwell
Moonlight and Starlight visit there
And the fresh bamboo forest form
a beautiful landscape with an aquamarine dream
I want to be there in Gan-a-dang

A white gourd flower builds a moon
A solomon's seal plays the coquette
A country spirit covers up the stepping stones
The bamboo scholars show their spirits
Lady Phallus Luteus appearing white
Where they write and recite poems, relaxing
I want to be in the land of Hermits

Where it is cozy like a mother's arms
Where it excites us like the first love

The red lamp lighting up at a cup of drink
When Sukhyang pours the drink with a scent of poems
I want to be there in Chuseong Village

[Samteo's Story]

Once, I sipped some drink
while staying at a cozy inn full of bamboo scent
in my old hometown, Damyang

The innkeeper was generous, and the food was decent
I got soaked in the scent of silently flowing poems
Staying up late, sipping drinks,
and chatting without noticing the flow of time
Until the place got blurred by the drinks
I stayed the night there

When I presented a poem
The innkeeper, such a nice wife she was
Posted my poem
on her wall

A Prayer of Blessing

Let me accomplish my dream
And become someone else's dream

Let me realize my true ideal
And become a milestone for someone else's dream

Give me peace through a harmonious energy of the sky
And let me dream a wise dream

Let me take a challenge with the burning energy of the sun
To reach the infinite world

Fill me up with love and care
Fill me up with Grace and happiness

Let me give thanks in all circumstances
And be filled with humble blessing

What a True Life is

A true life is
realizing that
all choices and decisions of being awake
are up to me

A true life is
the path that always shines with creativity
Where the light of wisdom shines our thoughts
so that we are filled with new energy

A true life is
becoming a protagonist who watches and listens
giving love voluntarily, not by his head but with his heart
That is the path you take

A Desperate Prayer of the New Year
– The song of peace for the country and its people

Happy New Year!
Let it be a year full of hope
Gain new energy from the sun
that rose up, lighting up the world

Stay healthy in this year
Let all your dreams be fulfilled
And let your life be filled with happiness and fortune

This year
Let the humanity's worries and hardships end
And let us see the end of the pandemic,
a fearful and severe disaster it was

This year
Let us recover the economy
that was shrunk and lost
Let us recover our health
and recover the relationships and problems

This year
Let us fill up our love and care for each other

Fill up the grace and happiness
And fill up our storages of disposable income

This year
Let us stabilize the politics and society
Trust will double up like a mother's milk
And justice will rise up like the burning sun
Righteous people will spread like a spring forest fire
And there will be peace for the country and its people

This year
Direct us with God's power
so public opinions can take action
Listen to the people's prayers and answer them
And fill our lives with abundance

The Time of Chaos

Long ago, three friends lived
One loved the river
Another loved the mountain
And the other loved the field
Where would they have a picnic?
They discussed, but could not reach an agreement
They want to head for a different place

The sky pretended ignorance
Heated up the world with burning tropical heat
Poured its rage on us
through thunder, lightning, rain, storm, and blizzard
Ruining the landscape and lyrics

Now, a mysterious creature called coronavirus
threatens the survival of humanity
And we are confused with ideologies
divided by race, religion, politics, and camps

Who made the standard for the humanity's yesterday and today?
Was it the gods?

Or the humans?
Where do life and death lead us to?
It's a lame sympathy
We sigh at the prophecy and myth

Divine Order

The power that keeps me
all night long, for 24 hours
is my dream

Every day
for 365 days a year
Love is the power that keeps me

The dream to bloom glittering flowers of poetry
The dream to bloom the flower of Nobel Prize
The dream to bloom a thousand-year-old flower
To collect the poetic ideas
To build concentration
To polish my love and dream
I only think of one thing

To love deeply
To love with my life
To love, looking up at my Divine Order

I Can Forgive You

It's you

It's only you

I will forget you

I cannot forget you

I love you

I leave you because I love you

I am dying of love for you

It's okay if it's a lie

It's autumn, anyway

It's a Beautiful Night

On a lonely night, while writing a poem
I come out to the yard and look at the full moon
I get soaked by the thought of you
The moon and stars are deep in thoughts
imagining countless things

The sun, moon, and stars
provide nutrients to the nature and creatures
I get to think
they're like my father's back and my mother's arms

Today, the ripe moon and stars
bringing us abundance
feel close and soft
like the beautiful arms of my darling

It's a beautiful night

Darling, Darling
– Love Song on a Thanksgiving Day

The night when the wind cannot fall asleep
The reed misses the autumn wind even in its sleep
And the lady longs for the scent of your poems

A scholar writes a letter, begging for your love
Confessing through a margin, like the ring around the moon
Saying that he loves you until death
He writes his poem

The reed field flowing along the autumn breeze
is soaked by the moon water
Moonlight falls on the nest that a musk deer loves

Grass bugs in the reed field are desperate to search love
My darling will come in my sleep
Today, I build a moon with tears again

Tears at the Beginning of the World

On a night dark like coal
When I shed tears, wetting my pillow
There's a ghost that appears in my head

On this silent night, I kneel and put my hands together
Hanging up the lamp that is leftover
And praying with meditation

The reason for my reflection
I pick up my brush with a poetic spirit
Touching the hologram desperately
To access the ghost

Even if we are lovers
Our thoughts can vary, I input
Shortening the distance between our thoughts
calls for sacrifice and care, I input
Reflect, I input

I sharpen my self-awareness
And put a knife on my incomplete character
Dead blood flowing from the mind and spirit of my

superego
All night long, I cut it off

When sunlight pours into my deep pond of thoughts
The ghost holding grudge wanders
until it becomes hot tears of the grass
and flows light blue

A Dreadful Dream

On a silent dawn
The ragged wound rots
The ghost burried in the public cemetry
gotten cold by the night
It wandered in the blank darkness, or the soil
and opened its eyes
But I did not see you
So I closed my eyes again

Outside the window, a sorrowful wind blows
The needle on my grandfather's clock
sounds sharp like a knife
Coming towards me
like the angel of death

When the red sunlight carries away the darkness
And ten thousand rays of sunlight
fixes a breakfast full of dream lights
Would I get to greet
your bright smile, my lover?

I cannot open my eyes, it's so dreadful

And the wound that has not healed up
Closes its eyes more tightly
And keeps on swimming
In the tough sea of darkness

Longing

The pain that lasts all night long
When stars fall asleep and dusk falls
Like dew setting off on a journey

Like the full moon
sunken in the moist dawn lake
Broken off by the river wind

Don't, Don't
The ripples that glitter despite ten-thousand hand waves

I thought I'd forgotten you, I thought I'd sent you
But you grasp my mind tight and seduce me

| Humor |

Part 6
Flapping the Skirt of the Robe

Autumn Pain

The sparse morning star falls asleep
And moonlight wets this dawn
Water mist that dwelled in the edge of flower lake
leaves with the breeze
Bird calls fix the breakfast

With the flap of the birds' wings
The flower petals that were barely holding on
fall on their bottoms, surprised

Summer leaves without a sound
And without noticing, autumn comes next to me
Can't go to sleep at the sound of crickets

It's just the autumn that comes every year
But this year, I feel sorrow in my deep heart
The dawn feels so long like a year

Cry, My Drink

The sky grants me a 'heavenly drink'
And the land drinks an 'earthly drink'

The landlord loves a drink
And the drink loves the landlord, creating heaven and earth
Dear all existences,
How could you reject a cup of drink?

Drink
Before the moonlit night cries
Drink, for this cup of drink
embraces the heaven and earth
Get drunk, and cry
Cry with the moonflower

When the ruddy drink wets my throat
I vomited trembling lust
My heart, wet with dew, burns hot
It is love in my heart

Apricot flowers bloom without a sound
A cuckoo cries without a tear

And love burns without smoke

I picked an Eastern prickly pear, for it was so beautiful
But its thorns poked my heart
I loved my friend, and talked of the world with him
But he gave a knife in my hands

I made friends with time, but it ran away on a horse
Wrinkles on my face formed a valley
Coming towards me with the Angel of Death on its back

Drink
When the starry night cries
Drink, for this cup of drink
embraces the heaven and earth
Get drunk, and cry
Starry night, you too, cry
Cry with the star flower

Market Day in Damyang
- The view of Manseong Bridge in Youngsan River

Where aquamarine soars up from the rapids
Whirlwind blowing in
Seven colors, a rainbow-colored water spray dreams

There's a marketplace along Youngsan River in Chuseong Village
Stalls of bamboo crafts
A boy is sitting on the stepping stones, painting with watercolors

Chinese minnows in the rapids
Wandong Village ladies carrying bamboo baskets and ironing their clothes
Colorful colors on the edge of their skirts
Weeping willows laugh

My sister's summer story
lying on the golden sand of summer
And the cool autumn breeze
brushes the tassels of a daffodil

I walk up the Gan-a-dang where water milfoils dance

A school of silvery flying fish embroiders the river
In the weed-bed, a hen and pheasant brood their eggs
And the chicks of a spotbill duck go for a swim

At the sound of the golden sunlight falling
The bamboo stalls of the marketplace close
And the bamboo leaf that flew from the boy's painting
skips in the river, with the autumn breeze

Flowers That Did Not Bloom
- The sorrowful Sewolho

See the petals falling
and flying away
Aren't they full of sorrow?

The dreams that barely bloomed
have sunken and are wandering in this world
Hear their desperate cries

The lives that are alive
will fade away with time
But what about those ghosts and spirits
that will never return?

The selfish pride and excuses
of the foolish, cold, little minds
The day of memorial becomes pale
Like those breaking waves

※ On the 2nd memorial of Sewolho incident

Flowers That Fell Before They Bloomed

Wind, stop blowing
Cruel waves, stop hitting
Don't be nasty, stop it
Stop shaking off
the flowers that fell before blooming

They are wandering in this world
What should we do with those little flowers?
The sky knows them
And we haven't yet forgotten them
What should we do, the Maengol waterway?

Killing those young souls one more time
The toxic knives of those devils
are gleaming again today

※ On the 2nd memorial of Sewolho incident

A Poet is a Martyr of Destroying Grammar

Human words operate
by delicate system called Grammar
This system is engraved in human brain
so delicately, that people do not perceive
that they follow it when they speak
But when you want to express things more precisely
Grammar comes out of your consciousness

Writing a poem
is a highly enhanced expression of your perception
and exposure of extremely delicate language
When a poet writes a poem,
he looks thoroughly into his own language
Sometimes, there is a gap between
the poetic spirit and the word he can express
He may have to make up a new word
or create a brand-new frame of sentence

In such cases, a poet destroys grammar on purpose
To put it correctly, this is not a destruction
It's a creation of new language
Therefore, a poet is a creator

and a leader who leads the development of language
However, if it doesn't involve the elevation of our spirits
or the suffering of destroying grammar
If it's merely a mistake of wrong spelling or word
It's a completely different problem

Before a poet can destroy a language,
he must be a worshipper of language
and an explorer of the mysterious world of language
He must try all he can to stay within the border
But at last, when he has to go over the border
He will destroy the old language with a firm determination
and create a fresh, new expression
He needs to commit to the development of language
Destruction without the determination to be a Martyr
is merely a wordplay

Dear Heaven, Dear Heaven
- Let us love

Biju, who came to the bus stop with a blue umbrella
greets her husband Jiyul
Imagining the scene that once thought had disappeared
brings joy and happiness to my heart

Rain becomes a stream and flows
It surges, almost coming into the street
When I get off the bus, my shoes are all wet
It almost reaches my calf
My license has been cancelled, so I took a taxi
But the driver stops the car far away from the street
I feel pity for my wet feet today

Stuck in the bed of my room, I turn on the TV
It's all news of heavy rain around the world

"Gangwon and Yeongnam will have 250mm of rain,
storm and lightning.
Honam and Jungbu will have over 200mm of
local rain.
The weather center predicted up to 200~250mm of rain
until dawn of 18th."

The Heaven seems thoughtless these days
When it was boiling hot, He closed His eyes
Did not spare a drop of rain
It seems there's a flood in the sky, too
As if He has opened the dam of heavenly water
It's pouring down

Dear Heaven,
Thoughtless Heaven,
Please don't take away our properties and lyrics
For the lives you have already taken
Let them sit on the best constellation of the Heaven

Please stop now
And pour us beautiful autumn light instead
Let the world be painted with lyrics
Let everyone enjoy the blessings
Let us love

Full Moon on Chuseok

I shed tears towards the western sky,
telling my sorrow without you in my day
Then the sky took away light so I can rest

I mumbled to the dark sky that I'm lonely
To light up your path of returning home
Countless star flowers bloomed

I cry out to the starry sky
That I miss you
Your face floated up

I begged you to love me
And from your swollen bosom
You pour down moon water

Swan

The sky is invited to the lake
And you're an angel floating like a cloud
You're a flower more beautiful
than the white water lily, the queen of flowers

When you become a solo ballerina
and dance across the aquamarine lake
The water lily's wide eyes envy you
And become a lake

A flower swimming along the waves
whiter than the white snow
You're a pure, white fairy

And water lily is the longing
that blooms a white flower
As you touch it
with your love

Moonlight Sonata

The silent darkness feels cold
Silence as dark as coal-black covers the wilderness
And I cannot see a thing

The white moonlight that makes the darkness sink
Time and space flying fast
Shivering fear hits
Plundering the pituitary gland
Attractive ecstasy
The shuddering, secret fear

Like the alluring poppy holding opium in its mouth
The frantic melody self-combusting with sensuality
jumping into the river
Acidifying and breaking off as an instance of aquamarine

Bouncing silence
And the mysterious moonlight surrounded by silence
The aquamarine of delight
permeating the heart and spirit of a poet

Long Life Alone

When I say that I'm lonely
Loneliness brings a whole gang of friends
Misfortune is never alone, it's a group
If you don't stop complaining about being lonely
The gang of loneliness will capture you
But if you keep walking your path without a complain
You will meet beautiful flowers on the road
and hear the birdsongs in the mountain

She, who entered the Silver Town after her husband's death
can't stop complaining that she's lonely
People gave her a nickname
A ridiculous nickname, 'At that time'
She always starts her sentence with it
"At that time, I traveled to warm places in winter.
At that time, I went hiking on weekends."
She only has past, not present
At 3 o' clock when the sunlight is bright
She seeks company to take a walk, but everyone avoids her
They're sick of her 'At that time' melody
Sometimes, I, the poet, go to the cinema or gallery

I do those things alone
To admire an artwork carefully
Alone is better, so I can concentrate with comfort
That day, I watched ⟨Safe Haven⟩
When I walked out of the cinema
A woman in my age talks to me

"Are you by yourself? Same here.
I come here about six times a month.
My daughter-in-law praises me for that,
but actually, I come here because I like it.
Today's movie was very impressive.
The young mother who is terminally ill
left a letter to a nameless woman
who may, later on, become a stepmother for her kids.
The letter was beautiful like a poem,
and it touched my heart."

Enjoy cultural life alone
It costs much less money than when you're with your friends
Take a walk alone, go to music concerts alone, and eat alone
Get used to being alone, and there's no time to feel lonely

Your body is the language of your heart

When you feel happy, your body feels happy
As seasons change and years pass, you will definitely age
But an elder who knows how to enjoy alone has a healthy body and mind
Everyone become alone at some point, and that's life
It's the era of drinking, eating, touring, watching movies, writing, and sleeping alone
Prepare for it from today
It's never too late

The Silver Grass Women

Their silvery tails dance uniformly
Musk deer in heat build a nest in their bosoms

Portraits drawn by the brown sunlight
Faint sadness glimmers in my eyes

On the silver grass field where sunset fell
A flock of white cranes are hugging, cheek to cheek
Through that flashy love game
Autumn wind breaks their hearts

When the waters of swollen full-moon breaks
The puddle in the silver grass field bears ripples

Brushing and tying the tails of white cranes
Embroidering the scent bag
Filling it up with the scent of musk deer
And hanging it on the coat string

Along the sound of the women
rubbing their scent bags
The scent of autumn ripens

[Quotations by Samteo]

I had childhood friends
who played in the silver grass field with me
picking silver grass and rolling on the ground

In that green nature
The kids' innocent memories
are the element and self-purifying power
that help us recover our nature
in this confusing culture of the city

Poem of a Smile

A smile is a pause, sprout, and sound
It's the breath within, a girl and boy
Bitter, sour, unfamiliar life

I summoned the smile without a sound
A soundless smile
An awkward bitter-smile
A sarcastic jeer-smile
A cynical cold-smile
An explosive laugh-out-loud smile
A collapsing uncontrollable smile
Laughing with claps, a roaring smile
With a grin, a broad smile

Smiling with your eyes
Laughing with a loud voice
With a whisper, a sneering smile
Simpering cold smile
A bitter smile
A forced smile
A snort
A wide smile

And a fake smile

Perhaps it's just a meaningless rumor
So I summon these smiles
It's just a belief or a gossip

Flapping the Skirt of the Robe

The robe, which my mother decorated with a collar, starched and ironed
With my father's dancing moves
Collects all the fun at Dongsu's garden party
Sweeping the whole house

Another day, my father visited a wedding at Wansu's place
Drinking and climbing up the afternoon moon
He flapped the skirt of his robe
and stepped out of the world for that one moment
Master of the drinks, he was
That's not it
He sat down on the ground with that white robe
And spilled the drink of rice wine
His robe got all wet

What should we do?
My baby sister Sunbok
pulled his arms and begged him to come home
My mother ran all the way to find him
"Honey, let's go home. Dinner has been fixed.

Come home and eat."

With my mom's rushing voice
The sun, who has been scratching its head
went over the hill
And the white dog wags his tail

Golden bats at the edge of our rafter are bustling
When the beautiful sunset decorates the sky bloody red
Dusk falls and the evening breeze gets cold
The gourd flower lady on our roof
digs up and plants the stars
Building a white moon over the roof
And lighting up the old house

Sinner

— Being woman is being a sinner

Born with the fate of a woman
You, born with the fate of a man
We lived half of our lives

As if our bodies have fulfilled its mission
The skin and bones are separated
In the crossroads
Dark black rain falls

Like a nameless cemetery
that collapses at a small rain
My heart flows as a black sin
without a lover in it

On the back of your drooping head
Only the remain of tearful, heavy, lost love
is clinging desperately

I try to ease my hunger
by drinking the soup of atonement
But you have let go of the string of life
Stretching out the torment of death

The sky which we have departed from
White cries of forgiveness fall
And grace sits on the ground
On the pink jacket of the apricot flowers
On the red skirt of the camellia
And on the bruised heart of the honeysuckle

But here I am now
Under the sky where I cannot heart those white cries
In need of more time to perceive and reflect
I'm a black woman who does not deserve forgiveness

The Lesson of Autumn

You need to drink a few cups
of clear spring water
The water that fills the autumn mountain
Drink, and wash it away

You need to lock it up in that wall
The lie, self-indulgence, love and hatred
On that red rope of arachne
Tie it up tightly

You need to let it go with sorrow
Erase the past and write it again
Empty it and fill a new today
Love your today

You need to give with a free hand
That's the lesson of autumn's abundance
Give, give again, and love

The Landscape of Fairyland

Water drips from the painting of the blue mountain
Did Jiyul fall asleep while painting the world of language?
Dark breeze blows in the bamboo forest
Rough strokes fly and dance on the painting

The drowsy dreams of the afternoon
have been erased by the black ink
The spirit of black bamboo
pushes away the white blank to the sky
Forming a magnificent blue

Jiyul, finished his reading of The Art of War last night, makes sorrowful eyes
A line made by the brush shows its bony frame
Expanding the time and space with its black texture
Seasons pass with each stroke

The red pine and blue bamboo in Jiyul's painting
pierced the blue sky, and rushing is gone
The painter, with a brush in his hands, is looking at the blue bamboo forest

And the afternoon moon is hanging on the bamboo leaves

A hexagonal gazebo is stretching its two legs
towards the water lily in the pond
A flute melody travels from the blue bamboo trees
Passing behind the painter's ears
Jiyul stays up all night long
The tears he shed last night are hanging on the petals
of the water lily

Into the livingroom where sunlight dwells
He walks in
The books in the square room
The lady bright like a sunlight running away through
the window
You can't hold a brush without a passion
The breeze blowing from the Juknokwon
carries the color of sorrow

SAEMMOON 1056

Dear Wind, From Flower

Lee Jung-rok 10th Poetry Collection

Issue_Nov. 1, 2024
Printing_Nov. 1, 2024
Publisher_Saemmoon Book Publishing
Author_Lee Jung-rok
Editing advisor_Lee Geun-bae, Kim So-yeop, Son Hae-il
Planning_Park Hoon-sik
Translator_Lee Sol
Design_Shin Sun-ok, Han Ga-eul
Printing_Saemmoon Book Publishing

Address_56 101gil   Dongil-ro Jungnang-gu, Seoul, Korea
Telephone_02-491-0060 / 02-491-0096
Fax_02-491-0040
E-mail_rok9539@daum.net / saemteonews@naver.com
Website_www.saemmoon.co.kr(Saem Literature)
         www.saemmoonnews.co.kr(Saemmoon News)
Publisher Registration_2019-26
Business Registration_113-82-76122
Saemmoon Literature Lifelong Educatin Center(Online Remote)-
Officially approved by Department of Education_320193122
Saemmoon Literature Lifelong Education Center(Offline)-
Officially approved by Department of Education_320203133

ISBN_979-11-94325-82-6

The formation of this poetry collection follows the author's intention.
Copyright of this book belongs to the author and Saemmoon.
Reprinting, plagiarism, and reproduction are strictly limited.

We offer an exchange of damaged books at the place of your purchase.
This book complies with the code of ethics and practice by the Korean publication ethics committee